The Big Question™

What does it take to make big impact?

Published by Adventurous Publishing
Copyright © 2024 Mark Walton

Paperback ISBN: 978-1-915862-62-4
Hardback ISBN: 978-1-915862-60-0

Welcome to this edition on

B!g impact

Ft MARK WALTON

International clients - LinkedIn

Contents

Tom Gaymor

OUR
WHY

The Big Question is a brand that delve's deep into the minds of influential leaders and uncover their strategies through asking Big questions.

We believe that the journey from aspiration to achievement is both fascinating and instructive.

By asking leaders profound questions about their experiences, we gain valuable insights that can guide you in turning your own dreams into tangible outcomes.

Welcome to this edition in The Big Question book series on Big impact.

In this book we speak to Mark Walton, the global client director at LinkedIn; in this book he shares recipes for big, positive impact and key steps to purpose finding, whilst touching on his journey.

Best,

-TBQ

Introduction

I'm Mark Walton, currently serving as the Global Client Director at LinkedIn.

In this role, I oversee relationships with some of our largest global clients while co-leading LinkedIn's Social Impact Board, which focuses on initiatives that support charities benefiting young people.

My journey to this point has been shaped by a blend of personal experiences, career shifts, and a commitment to making a meaningful difference.

This book is a reflection on what it takes to create a significant impact, drawing from my own experiences and broader observations on the power of purposeful action.

Chapter one

Just a boy from margate

My story begins in Margate, Kent, where I grew up in a working-class family. Despite a loving and stable upbringing, financial constraints were a constant challenge. I vividly recall the stress that financial limitations imposed on my family, particularly on my father, who worked hard to provide for us.

Our reliance on hand-me-down clothes highlighted the economic difficulties we faced, shaping my early understanding of resilience and empathy.

These early experiences profoundly impacted my worldview, instilling a deep sense of compassion for those in similar situations.

They also sparked a desire to bridge gaps for others facing similar hardships.

As a child, my dreams were firmly set on becoming a professional footballer. The excitement and camaraderie of sports fueled my aspirations. However, as I matured, my career ambitions began to evolve.

Influenced by my grandfather's stories and his own service in the RAF, I contemplated a military career. This period of exploration was pivotal, helping me recognize the importance of aligning career choices with personal values and interests.

Ultimately, my journey took a significant turn when I pursued a law degree. This decision was initially driven by a desire to understand complex systems and advocate effectively.

However, it was during this academic period that I discovered a passion for sales—a field that offered dynamic interaction and strategic challenges.

Over the past 25 years, I've focused on sales, continually refining my approach and discovering what truly drives me.

Chapter two

My mentors - the roles they play

Throughout my life, several mentors have profoundly influenced me. My grandfather on my mother's side stands out as a beacon of kindness and resilience.

His values and principles have guided my personal and professional endeavors, offering a model of integrity and perseverance.

In my professional journey, mentors like Mike—who emphasized respect and equality—and leaders at LinkedIn—who introduced conscious business principles—have shaped my approach to leadership and social impact.

Their guidance has reinforced the importance of ethical practices and a commitment to making a positive difference.

In my role as Global Client Director at LinkedIn, I lead a team dedicated to working with senior HR leaders to help organizations attract and develop talent. By leveraging innovative HR software solutions and analytics platforms, we enhance talent acquisition and development strategies.

This role enables me to contribute to the success of global organizations by fostering impactful partnerships and delivering tailored solutions.

My involvement with LinkedIn's Social Impact Board is particularly fulfilling. Our initiatives aim to support young people through various programs, including mentoring and partnerships with youth-focused charities.

These efforts are deeply rooted in my own childhood experiences and the challenges I faced. I am committed to bridging gaps and providing opportunities that I missed out on, which has been a source of great personal and professional satisfaction.

Our mentoring programs have made a significant difference, offering guidance and confidence to countless young individuals.

Collaborations with charities have allowed us to extend our impact, providing essential skills, educational opportunities, and pathways to meaningful employment. Witnessing these transformations reinforces the importance of our work and the power of collective efforts in driving positive change.

Chapter Three

Finding your purpose

Finding your purpose is often described as one of life's most profound quests. It is a journey of introspection and discovery, a process that involves delving deep into your values, passions, and unique abilities.

This quest for purpose is not merely about identifying a career path or setting professional goals; it's about understanding what truly motivates and fulfills you on a fundamental level.

Purpose acts as a compass, guiding you through the complexities of life and career decisions. It provides clarity, focus, and direction, transforming challenges into opportunities for growth and fulfillment.

But how does one embark on this journey?
How do you uncover the underlying principles that will guide your actions and decisions?

The first step in finding your purpose is to reflect on your personal experiences. Start by examining the moments in your life that have been most meaningful to you.

What activities or experiences have brought you the greatest joy and satisfaction? Consider both your professional achievements and personal milestones. Reflect on times when you felt most alive and engaged, and think about what these moments have in common.

It is also helpful to analyze the challenges you have faced and the lessons learned from them. Often, our struggles and setbacks can offer valuable insights into what we are truly passionate about and what we want to stand for.

Reflecting on these experiences can help you understand what drives you, what you value, and what kind of impact you want to make in the world.

As you continue on this journey, remember that your purpose is not a destination but a dynamic and evolving process.

Embrace the exploration, remain committed to your goals, and stay open to the transformative power of aligning your life with what truly matters to you.

Chapter Four

Creating big impact

Creating a big impact is not a singular event but rather a continuous journey. It involves aligning your personal experiences and passions with purposeful action. For me, the journey has been deeply intertwined with my role at LinkedIn and my commitment to supporting young people through various social impact initiatives. I

've learned that making a significant difference requires more than just grand gestures; it involves a series of deliberate, purposeful steps.

My journey toward creating a big impact began with a reflection on my personal experiences and passions. Growing up in Margate, Kent, with financial constraints, I developed a deep empathy for those facing similar challenges.

This personal understanding of struggle became a driving force behind my professional and philanthropic efforts. I've always believed that our experiences, whether positive or negative, shape our understanding of the world and our desire to effect change.

As I reflect on my career, transitioning from dreams of becoming a professional footballer to pursuing law and finally finding my calling in sales, I see how each shift was influenced by my passion for connection and impact.

It was in sales that I discovered a platform to influence change on a larger scale, allowing me to use my skills to help others achieve their goals.

identifying a clear purpose has been a cornerstone of my journey. My involvement with LinkedIn's Social Impact Board has given me a platform to channel my purpose into meaningful initiatives. We focus on supporting charities that benefit young people, and this mission is deeply rooted in my own childhood experiences.

By aligning my professional role with my personal values, I've been able to drive impactful change both within LinkedIn and through our external partnerships.

For me, purpose is about finding that intersection between what you're passionate about and what the world needs. It's about identifying where your skills and experiences can make a meaningful difference.

At LinkedIn, our purpose is to create economic opportunities for every member of the global workforce. By connecting this purpose with my own experiences and values, I've been able to make a more significant impact.

One of the key lessons I've learned is the importance of leveraging resources and networks. At LinkedIn, we have access to extensive tools, technologies, and a vast network of professionals. Utilizing these resources effectively can amplify your impact.

For instance, our mentoring programs and partnerships with youth-focused charities leverage LinkedIn's platform to provide young people with skills, educational opportunities, and employment pathways.

Building and maintaining strong networks has been essential in scaling our impact. By collaborating with other organizations and individuals who share our vision, we've been able to extend our reach and effectiveness.

Networking isn't just about making connections; it's about forging meaningful partnerships that enhance your ability to drive change.

Taking action is where the real impact happens. It's one thing to have a purpose and access resources, but translating that into concrete results requires deliberate effort. I've learned that persistence is crucial.

The journey to making a big impact is filled with challenges and setbacks. There were times when our initiatives faced obstacles, whether logistical or financial, but staying committed to our mission and continuously pushing forward made all the difference.

Persistence means not only overcoming immediate challenges but also continually adapting and evolving. It's about being willing to adjust your strategies and approaches based on what you learn along the way.

In our mentoring programs, for example, we've made adjustments based on feedback and outcomes to better meet the needs of young people and ensure that our support remains relevant and effective.

Finally, measuring impact and being willing to adapt is essential for sustained success. At LinkedIn, we continuously assess the effectiveness of our social impact initiatives.

We track metrics such as the number of youths mentored, their educational achievements, and their employment outcomes. This data helps us understand what's working and where we need to make improvements.

Adaptation is about being responsive to the needs of those we aim to help and the evolving landscape of our work. It involves analyzing outcomes, gathering feedback, and making informed adjustments to our strategies.

For instance, if a particular program isn't delivering the desired results, we analyze why and make necessary changes to enhance its effectiveness.

Creating a big impact is a journey of aligning personal experiences and passions with purposeful action. It involves reflecting on your experiences, identifying a clear purpose, leveraging resources and networks, taking persistent action, and continuously measuring and adapting.

Each of these elements contributes to making a meaningful difference in the world.

For you, the reader, consider how you can apply these principles to your own life and work. Reflect on your experiences, identify your purpose, leverage your resources and networks, take decisive action, and measure your impact.

By doing so, you can create a significant and lasting difference in the areas that matter most to you.

Your journey starts with understanding your values and passions and translating them into purposeful action.

Embrace the journey, stay committed, and make your mark on the world.

My big question to you is..

***What** will you do to make a positive impact on the world?*

About the author

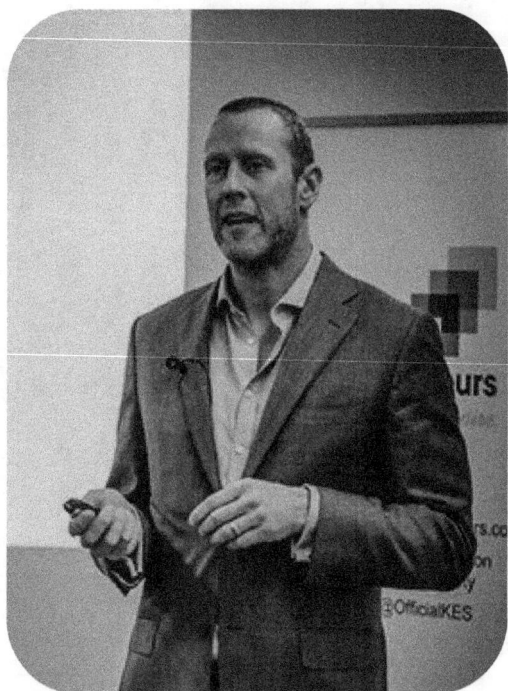

Mark walton works with LinkedIn's largest & most strategic global clients, to drive their business growth through talent strategies that are human led & tech enabled.

He leads a global, cross functional team, that partners with clients as well as HR leadership teams to help them deliver their strategic business objectives.

Be you,
be bold,
Go big.

-TBQ

NOTES

THE B!G QUESTION.

_____

_____

_____

_____

_____

_____

_____

_____

_____

_____

_____

_____

_____

_____

_____

_____..............Go big

THE B!G QUESTION.

_____
_____
_____
_____
_____
_____
_____
_____
_____
_____
_____
_____
_____
_____
_____
_____
_____
..........GO B!G

THE B!G QUESTION.

_____

_____

_____

_____

_____

_____

_____

_____

_____

_____

_____

_____

_____

_____

_____............GO B!G

THE B!G QUESTION.

_____

_____

_____

_____

_____

_____

_____

_____

_____

_____

_____

_____

_____

_____

_____

_____

............GO B!G

THE B!G QUESTION.

_____
_____
_____
_____
_____
_____
_____
_____
_____
_____
_____
_____
_____
_____
_____
_____...........GO B!G

THE B!G QUESTION.

_____
_____
_____
_____
_____
_____
_____
_____
_____
_____
_____
_____
_____
_____
_____
_____
_____............GO B!G

THE B!G QUESTION.

_____
_____
_____
_____
_____
_____
_____
_____
_____
_____
_____
_____
_____
_____
_____
_____
...........GO B!G

THE B!G QUESTION.

_____

_____

_____

_____

_____

_____

_____

_____

_____

_____

_____

_____

_____

_____

...........GO B!G

THE B!G QUESTION.

_____
_____
_____
_____
_____
_____
_____
_____
_____
_____
_____
_____
_____
_____
_____
_____
_____
.............GO B!G
_____

THE B!G QUESTION.

_____
_____
_____
_____
_____
_____
_____
_____
_____
_____
_____
_____
_____
_____
_____
_____
............GO B!G

THE B!G QUESTION.

_____
_____
_____
_____
_____
_____
_____
_____
_____
_____
_____
_____
_____
_____
_____
_____
_____
_____
_____............GO B!G

THE B!G QUESTION.

_____

_____

_____

_____

_____

_____

_____

_____

_____

_____

_____

_____

_____

_____

_____

.............GO B!G

THE B!G QUESTION.

_____
_____
_____
_____
_____
_____
_____
_____
_____
_____
_____
_____
_____
_____
_____
_____
_____
_____............GO B!G

THE B!G QUESTION.

_____
_____
_____
_____
_____
_____
_____
_____
_____
_____
_____
_____
_____
_____
_____
_____
_____............GO B!G

THE B!G QUESTION.

_____
_____
_____
_____
_____
_____
_____
_____
_____
_____
_____
_____
_____
_____
_____
_____
_____............GO B!G

THE B!G QUESTION.

_____
_____
_____
_____
_____
_____
_____
_____
_____
_____
_____
_____
_____
_____
_____
_____
_____
_____
_____...........GO B!G

THE B!G QUESTION.

_____

_____

_____

_____

_____

_____

_____

_____

_____

_____

_____

_____

_____

_____

_____...........GO B!G

THE B!G QUESTION.

_____
_____
_____
_____
_____
_____
_____
_____
_____
_____
_____
_____
_____
_____
............GO B!G

THE B!G QUESTION.

_____
_____
_____
_____
_____
_____
_____
_____
_____
_____
_____
_____
_____
_____
_____
_____
_____
_____
_____
.............GO B!G

THE B!G QUESTION.

_____
_____
_____
_____
_____
_____
_____
_____
_____
_____
_____
_____
_____
_____
_____
_____
_____
_____
_____............GO B!G

in	The Big Question
⃝	@thebigquestionhq
✉	thebigquestioninfo@gmail.com

" GO B!G...

www.ingramcontent.com/pod-product-compliance
Lightning Source LLC
LaVergne TN
LVHW022013080426
835513LV00009B/691